Girls Play
SOFTBALL

Girls JOIN THE TEAM

Amy B. Rogers

New York

Published in 2017 by The Rosen Publishing Group, Inc.
29 East 21st Street, New York, NY 10010

First Edition

Editor: Katie Kawa
Book Design: Tanya Dellaccio

Photo Credits: Cover Guang Niu/Getty Images; p. 5 Andy Cross/The Denver Post/ Getty Images; p. 7 (top) MIGUEL GUTIERREZ/AFP/Getty Images; p. 7 (bottom) Mark Rucker/Transcendental Graphics/Getty Images; p. 11 John Biever/Sports Illustrated/ Getty Images; pp. 13 (top), 17 Clive Rose/Getty Images; p. 13 (bottom) Jan de Wild/ Shutterstock.com; p. 15 (top) Doug Jones/Portland Press Herald/Getty Images; p. 15 (bottom) Doug Hoke/Time Life Pictures/Getty Images; p. 16 Vladimir Rys/ Bongarts/Getty Images; p. 18 Matthew Stockman/Getty Images; p. 19 Al Bello/Getty Images; p. 21 Diamond Images/Getty Images; p. 22 bikeriderlondon/Shutterstock.com.

Cataloging-in-Publication Data

Names: Rogers, Amy B.
Title: Girls play softball / Amy B. Rogers.
Description: New York : PowerKids Press, 2017. | Series: Girls join the team | Includes index.
Identifiers: ISBN 9781508149644 (pbk.) | ISBN 9781499421095 (library bound) | ISBN 9781499421088 (6 pack)
Subjects: LCSH: Softball for women–Juvenile literature. | Softball for children–Juvenile literature.
Classification: LCC GV881.3 R64 2017 | DDC 796.357'8082-d23

Manufactured in the United States of America

CPSIA Compliance Information: Batch #BS16PK For Further Information contact Rosen Publishing, New York, New York at 1-800-237-9932

CONTENTS

TAKE ME OUT TO THE BALL GAME!

Amazing home runs, speedy steals, and strong defense—these are just some of the exciting parts of a softball game. Softball is a lot like baseball, but there are some important differences. The ball is bigger, the field is smaller, and the games have fewer innings. Also, baseball pitchers throw the ball overhand, while softball pitchers throw underhand.

While men can play softball, it's become very popular among women and girls. Girls sometimes begin playing softball even before they go to kindergarten. As they grow into great softball players, they learn how to **focus** and how to work hard for a big win!

Overtime!

There are two main kinds of softball: slow-pitch and fast-pitch. The speed of the pitches is the biggest difference between the two. Also, in slow-pitch softball, you can't steal bases, or advance to the next base while the pitcher is throwing the ball. You can steal when playing fast-pitch.

Many communities have their own softball teams and **leagues**. If this sport sounds like fun, it's never too early—or too late—to start playing!

SOFTBALL'S BEGINNINGS

Softball started in the United States. It's generally accepted that the first softball game was played in 1887 in Chicago, Illinois. A reporter named George Hancock is often credited with inventing the sport.

The Amateur Softball Association (ASA) was formed in 1933 to govern the sport in the United States. Its headquarters are in Oklahoma City, Oklahoma. In 1952, the International Softball Federation (ISF) was created to connect softball-playing countries around the world. It hosts international **competitions**, including world **championships**. The United States sent its first softball team to an ISF Women's World Championship in 1965. That team won a silver **medal**.

Overtime!

From 1943 to 1954, women were given the opportunity to play **professional** baseball through the All-American Girls Professional Baseball League. The women who played in this league helped pave the way for today's softball players and other female athletes.

Today, the ISF governs softball in more than 120 countries around the world!

All-American Girls Professional Baseball League team in 1945

ON THE DIAMOND

A softball field is sometimes called a diamond because of its shape. Like a baseball diamond, it has four bases: first base, second base, third base, and home plate. Home plate is where the batter stands, and it's what a base runner has to touch in order to score a run. The team with the most runs at the end of a softball game wins.

The batter's job is to hit the ball with her bat after the pitcher throws it to her. Players on the team that's at bat, or trying to hit the ball, try to move all the way around the bases to score a run when the ball is hit and not caught in the air.

Overtime!

A softball diamond is divided into two main parts. The infield is the part of the diamond around the bases. The outfield is the part beyond the infield. The infield is most often dirt, while the outfield is grass.

Playing the Field

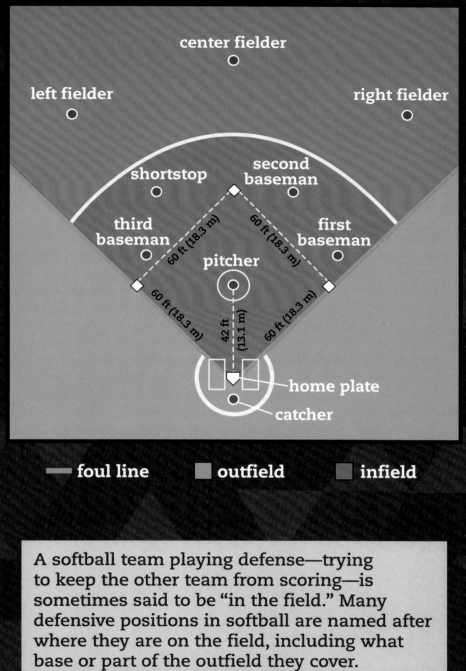

A softball team playing defense—trying to keep the other team from scoring—is sometimes said to be "in the field." Many defensive positions in softball are named after where they are on the field, including what base or part of the outfield they cover.

THREE STRIKES OR A HOME RUN?

When a softball player is at bat, she generally gets three tries to hit the ball. A strike happens when a batter swings and misses the ball. A foul ball can also be a strike. A foul ball happens when the ball is hit over one of the foul lines on the sides of the field. In most cases, a foul ball can't be a third strike.

If a player hits the ball, she has to run to first base. She can also keep running on to the next bases if she thinks she can make it there safely. That means making it there before a defensive player touches, or tags, her with the ball.

Overtime!

If a softball player hits the ball far enough to be able to run to all the bases, she's hit a home run. A grand slam is a home run when the bases are loaded, or when there are players standing on all the bases. Those players all get to cross home plate, scoring four runs with one hit!

Sometimes a base runner has to slide into the base to avoid getting tagged.

YOU'RE OUT!

If a batter gets three strikes or a base runner gets tagged, it's called an out. An out can also happen if a defensive player holding the ball touches the base before the base runner reaches it. This only causes an out if the runner is forced to move to that base, because there can't be two players on the same base. Another way to get an out is to catch the ball in the air after it's hit. After the players in the field make three outs, they get their turn at bat.

An inning in a softball game occurs when both teams have a chance to bat and play in the field. There are seven innings in a softball game.

Overtime!

Softball players wear important safety gear, including a helmet when they bat. Many softball players also wear a mouth guard, as well as special pads to **protect** their legs. Certain softball players, especially catchers, wear masks to protect their face, as well as chest protectors.

Pitchers are important players on any softball team. They can get strikeouts for their team by making players from the other team swing at the ball and miss three times. Monica Abbott holds the record for the most strikeouts in a college softball **career** with 2,440.

Monica Abbott

WINNING THE WCWS

In 1972, a law called Title IX, or Title Nine, was passed. This law states schools that get funding from the **federal** government have to give girls and women the same opportunity to play sports as boys and men. This law allowed women's sports programs to grow in colleges and high schools across the United States. Softball soon became a major college sport for women to play and for everyone to watch.

The Women's College World Series (WCWS) is the yearly college softball championship in the United States. Games are played between 64 teams, and all the games are shown on national television.

Overtime!

The University of California, Los Angeles (UCLA), has been the college with the most successful women's softball program in the United States. Since 1982, UCLA's softball team has won 12 college softball championships.

UCLA's
Lisa Fernandez

Almost 300 colleges are **eligible** for the WCWS. College softball players have to work hard on the field and in the classroom.

TEAM USA

For many years, young softball players dreamed of playing for their country at the Summer Olympics. Softball became an Olympic sport in 1996. The United States won the first three gold medals for the sport, and Team USA won a silver medal in 2008. Softball was then removed from Olympic competition, although many are working hard to bring the sport back to the Summer Olympics.

Now, the most famous international competition for softball players is the World Cup of Softball. As of 2015, the United States has won the World Cup of Softball eight out of the 10 times the event has been held.

Overtime!

One of the most famous hitters in Olympic softball history is Crystl Bustos. During the 2008 Summer Olympics, Crystl hit a record six home runs while playing for Team USA!

The World Cup of Softball has drawn record-breaking crowds and television viewers for an international softball competition. Many hope the popularity of this event will prove that softball should once again be included in the Summer Olympics.

JENNIE AND JESSICA

One of the most famous members of Team USA when softball was an Olympic sport was Jennie Finch. Jennie's a pitcher who had a 2-0 record in the 2004 Summer Olympics, helping Team USA win gold. She was also on the 2008 team that won silver. Jennie works hard to keep the sport growing by holding softball camps to teach young girls the game.

One of Jennie's teammates at the 2004 and 2008 Olympics was Jessica Mendoza. After Jessica's softball career ended, she began to cover baseball and softball as an **analyst** on national television.

Overtime!

In 2015, Jessica Mendoza became the first female analyst to cover a Major League Baseball game for the popular television network ESPN.

Jennie and Jessica continue to work as hard off the softball diamond as they did on it. They're both involved in the Women's Sports Foundation, and they want to **inspire** girls to become not just the best softball players they can be, but the best women they can be.

Jennie Finch

PROFESSIONAL SOFTBALL

Both Jennie and Jessica—as well as many of their Olympic teammates—also played softball professionally. National Pro Fastpitch (NPF) is the professional softball league for women in the United States. This league began as the Women's Pro Softball League in 1997, but that league only lasted until 2001.

Professional softball returned in 2004 with NPF. This league features the game's brightest stars and allows fans to see softball played at the highest level. Some NPF games—including the league championship—are shown on national television. NPF players help their sport grow by doing all they can to connect with their fans.

Overtime!

The best softball pitchers can throw the ball at speeds of more than 75 miles (120.7 km) per hour!

Girls who play softball can grow up dreaming of a professional career playing the sport they love because of NPF!

SUCCEEDING ON AND OFF THE DIAMOND

Around the world, girls are growing into stronger, smarter women through the sport of softball. This is especially true in the United States, where softball diamonds are part of most communities. Also, more girls are able to watch this sport at different levels than ever before—thanks to increased television coverage for softball games such as the WCWS.

If you play softball, you'll learn valuable skills that will help you succeed not just on the diamond, but in all areas of life. If you work hard enough, you might find yourself playing in the WCWS or for the NPF championship!

GLOSSARY

analyst: A person who is skilled in studying a topic and is sometimes asked to speak about that topic.

career: A period of time spent doing a job or activity.

championship: A contest to find out who's the best player or team in a sport.

competition: An event between two or more people or groups to find a winner.

eligible: Able to be chosen or to participate.

federal: Relating to the central government of the United States.

focus: Directed attention.

inspire: To move someone to do something great.

league: A group of teams that play the same sport and compete against each other.

medal: A flat, small piece of metal with art or words that's used as an honor or reward.

professional: Having to do with a job someone does for a living.

protect: To keep safe.

INDEX

WEBSITES

Due to the changing nature of Internet links, PowerKids Press has developed
an online list of websites related to the subject of this book. This site is
updated regularly. Please use this link to access the list:
www.powerkidslinks.com/gjt/sball